Haldane

by Iain Gray

79 Main Street, Newtongrange,
Midlothian EH22 4NA
Tel: 0131 344 0414   Fax: 0845 075 6085
E-mail: info@lang-syne.co.uk
www.langsyneshop.co.uk

Design by Dorothy Meikle
Printed by Printwell Ltd
© Lang Syne Publishers Ltd 2021

All rights reserved. No part of this publication may be reproduced, stored or introduced into a retrieval system, or transmitted in any form or by any means (electronic, mechanical, photocopying, recording or otherwise) without the prior written permission of Lang Syne Publishers Ltd.

ISBN 978-1-85217-761-4

Haldane

MOTTO:
Suffer

CREST:
The head of an eagle

TERRITORIES:
Perthshire, Stirlingshire

NAME variations include:
Hadden
Haldean
Halden
Haldenby
Haldin

Chapter one:

The origins of the clan system

by Rennie McOwan

The original Scottish clans of the Highlands and the great families of the Lowlands and Borders were gatherings of families, relatives, allies and neighbours for mutual protection against rivals or invaders.

Scotland experienced invasion from the Vikings, the Romans and English armies from the south. The Norman invasion of what is now England also had an influence on land-holding in Scotland. Some of these invaders stayed on and in time became 'Scottish'.

The word clan derives from the Gaelic language term 'clann', meaning children, and it was first used many centuries ago as communities were formed around tribal lands in glens and mountain fastnesses.

The format of clans changed over the centuries, but at its best the chief and his family held the land on behalf of all, like trustees, and the ordinary clansmen and women believed they had a blood relationship with the founder of their clan.

There were two way duties and obligations. An inadequate chief could be deposed and replaced by someone of greater ability.

Clan people had an immense pride in race. Their relationship with the chief was like adult children to a father and they had a real dignity.

The concept of clanship is very old and a more feudal notion of authority gradually crept in.

Pictland, for instance, was divided into seven principalities ruled by feudal leaders who were the strongest and most charismatic leaders of their particular groups.

By the sixth century the 'British' kingdoms of Strathclyde, Lothian and Celtic Dalriada (Argyll) had emerged and Scotland, as one nation, began to take shape in the time of King Kenneth MacAlpin.

Some chiefs claimed descent from ancient kings which may not have been accurate in every case.

By the twelfth and thirteenth centuries the clans and families were more strongly brought under the central control of Scottish monarchs.

Lands were awarded and administered more and more under royal favour, yet the power of the area clan chiefs was still very great.

The long wars to ensure Scotland's

independence against the expansionist ideas of English monarchs extended the influence of some clans and reduced the lands of others.

Those who supported Scotland's greatest king, Robert the Bruce, were awarded the territories of the families who had opposed his claim to the Scottish throne.

In the Scottish Borders country – the notorious Debatable Lands – the great families built up a ferocious reputation for providing warlike men accustomed to raiding into England and occasionally fighting one another.

Chiefs had the power to dispense justice and to confiscate lands and clan warfare produced a society where martial virtues – courage, hardiness, tenacity – were greatly admired.

Gradually the relationship between the clans and the Crown became strained as Scottish monarchs became more orientated to life in the Lowlands and, on occasion, towards England.

The Highland clans spoke a different language, Gaelic, whereas the language of Lowland Scotland and the court was Scots and in more modern times, English.

Highlanders dressed differently, had different

customs, and their wild mountain land sometimes seemed almost foreign to people living in the Lowlands.

It must be emphasised that Gaelic culture was very rich and story-telling, poetry, piping, the clarsach (harp) and other music all flourished and were greatly respected.

Highland culture was different from other parts of Scotland but it was not inferior or less sophisticated.

Central Government, whether in London or Edinburgh, sometimes saw the Gaelic clans as a challenge to their authority and some sent expeditions into the Highlands and west to crush the power of the Lords of the Isles.

Nevertheless, when the eighteenth century Jacobite Risings came along the cause of the Stuarts was mainly supported by Highland clans.

The word Jacobite comes from the Latin for James – Jacobus. The Jacobites wanted to restore the exiled Stuarts to the throne of Britain.

The monarchies of Scotland and England became one in 1603 when King James VI of Scotland (1st of England) gained the English throne after Queen Elizabeth died.

The Union of Parliaments of Scotland and England, the Treaty of Union, took place in 1707.

Some Highland clans, of course, and Lowland families opposed the Jacobites and supported the incoming Hanoverians.

After the Jacobite cause finally went down at Culloden in 1746 a kind of ethnic cleansing took place. The power of the chiefs was curtailed. Tartan and the pipes were banned in law.

Many emigrated, some because they wanted to, some because they were evicted by force. In addition, many Highlanders left for the cities of the south to seek work.

Many of the clan lands became home to sheep and deer shooting estates.

But the warlike traditions of the clans and the great Lowland and Border families lived on, with their descendants fighting bravely for freedom in two world wars.

Remember the men from whence you came, says the Gaelic proverb, and to that could be added the role of many heroic women.

The spirit of the clan, of having roots, whether Highland or Lowland, means much to thousands of people.

Meanwhile, many families proudly boast the heraldic device known as a Coat of Arms,.

The central motif of the Coat of Arms would originally have been what was sometimes borne on the shield of a warrior to distinguish himself from others on the battlefield.

Clan warfare produced a society where courage and tenacity were greatly admired

Chapter two:

In freedom's cause

Meaning 'Half-Dane', the Haldane name suggests a possible rich and heady brew of the blood of Scandinavians and Gaels may run through the veins of its bearers today.

Norsemen such as the Vikings and Scandinavian Danes first began their bloody incursions into Scotland in the eighth century, but many eventually abandoned their feared long ships in favour of settlement – intermixing with the native race.

But another possible derivation of the name is that it may be of territorial designation, with the family that became known as the Haldanes taking it from the lands in which they were settled.

Lending credence to this theory is that between 1165 and 1171, during the reign of King William I, better known as William the Lion, a 'Bernard, son of Brien', was granted the manor of 'Hauden' – a name that phonetically bears a striking similarity to 'Haldane.'

It was a cadet branch of this family, settled in

Strathearn, Perthshire, who became known as 'Haldane', or by one of its now redundant spelling variants – and, for the sake of consistency in this narrative of the family, 'Haldane' is the form henceforth adopted.

Granted the barony of 'Glen Eagles', more commonly rendered as 'Gleneagles', the chieftainship of the clan rested on them – as it does to this day.

'Glen Eagles' known in Gaelic as *Gleann na h-Eaglais /Gleann Eagas*, refers to the glen that, connecting with Glen Devon, forms a pass through the Ochil Hills.

'Eagles', surprisingly, does not refer to the magnificent bird of prey of the name, but is a corruption of the Gaelic eaglais, or ecclesia, indicating 'church' – and the church in question refers to the chapel and well of St Mungo that, now renovated, stands as a memorial to the Haldane family.

Gleneagles House on the Gleneagles estate – and separate from the privately-owned and internationally famous Gleneagles Hotel – is the seat of Clan Haldane, while another seat is Airthrey Castle, Stirlingshire – and of which more later.

The first real historical figure to step onto the pages of the Haldane saga is Almer (or Aylmer)

Haldane of Gleneagles – making his appearance at a pivotal time in Scotland's fraught relationship with England.

This was as one of the signatories at Berwick in 1296 to a humiliating treaty of fealty to England's conquering King Edward I, known as the Hammer of the Scots.

Signed – albeit reluctantly – by 1,500 Scottish earls, bishops and burgesses, the parchment is known as the *Ragman Roll* because of the profusion of ribbons that dangle from the seals of the signatories.

Scotland had been thrown into crisis ten years earlier with the death of King Alexander II and the death four years later of his successor, the Maid of Norway, who died while en route to Scotland to take up the crown.

John Balliol was controversially enthroned at Scone as King of Scots in 1292 – but fatefully for the nation they had asked the powerful and ambitious King Edward I to arbitrate in the bitter dispute over the succession to the throne, and the hapless Balliol had found himself the English king's chosen man.

The Scots rose in revolt against his imperialist designs in July of 1296 but the ruthless monarch brought the entire nation under his subjugation less than a month later, garrisoning strategic locations throughout the length and breadth of the nation, and demanding the signing of the *Ragman Roll*.

But subjugation under the iron fist of English occupation did not sit well with the proud Scots, and the great patriot William Wallace raised the banner of revolt in May of 1297.

A charismatic leader and an expert in the tactics of guerrilla warfare, Wallace and his hardened band of freedom fighters set Scotland aflame – boosting the morale of their fellow countrymen as they inflicted a stunning series of defeats on the English garrisons.

This culminated in the liberation of practically all of Scotland following the battle of Stirling Bridge, on September 11, 1297.

But, defeated at the battle of Falkirk on July 22, 1298, after earlier being appointed Guardian of Scotland, Sir William Wallace was eventually betrayed and captured seven years later, and was brutally executed in London as a 'traitor' on August 23, 1305.

His execution only served to further inflame Scottish patriotism, however, and the cause of the nation's freedom was taken up again, this time under the inspired leadership of the great warrior king

Robert the Bruce, who had been enthroned as king at Scone in March of 1306.

Over the next eight long years, Bruce and his band of loyal supporters – who included Almer Haldane – enjoyed an astonishing series of successes that left the occupying English forces reeling and culminated in Bruce's decisive victory over the army of Edward's successor, Edward II, at the battle of Bannockburn in midsummer of 1314.

In 1312, two years before Bannockburn, Almer Haldane's kinsman Sir Simon Haldane had added to the family's land holdings when he received a charter for part of the lands of Bardrill, in Strathearn and, through his marriage to Matilda de Arnot, lands that lay within the earldom of Lennox.

His successor as Chief of Clan Haldane, Sir John Haldane, third of Gleneagles, married Agnes, daughter of Murdoch Menteith of Rusky and, through this claimed the earldom of Lennox – held by Stuart, Lord Darnley.

A complex and lengthy lawsuit between the two powerful magnates ensued, but it was settled when it was agreed Lord Darnley retain the earldom and Haldane compensated with the grant of a substantial proportion of the Lennox lands.

Sir John Haldane, meanwhile, held high office as Master of the Household under King James III, Lord Justice General of Scotland beyond the Forth and sheriff principal of Edinburgh.

Resigning lands he held to the Crown, he in turn received a charter that gave him the status of holder of the free barony of Gleneagles.

In 1505, Sir James Haldane, fourth of Gleneagles, was appointed governor of the strategically important bastion of Dunbar Castle while, under his son Sir John Haldane, fifth of Gleneagles, family lands in Lennox and Perthshire that were not at that point part of the Gleneagles barony were given the status of the barony of Haldane.

But loyalty to the Crown and the rewards that accordingly accrued often came at great cost, with Sir John Haldane among the 5,000 Scots including James IV, an archbishop, two bishops, eleven earls, fifteen barons, and 300 knights killed at the disastrous battle of Flodden on September 9, 1513.

The Scottish monarch had embarked on the venture after Queen Anne of France, under the terms of the Auld Alliance between Scotland and her nation, appealed to him to 'break a lance' on her behalf and act as her chosen knight.

Crossing the border into England at the head of a 25,000-strong army that included 7,500 clansmen and their kinsmen, James engaged a 20,000-strong force commanded by the Earl of Surrey – but despite their numerical superiority and bravery, the Scots proved no match for the skilled English artillery and superior military tactics of Surrey.

Chapter three:

Crown and Covenant

In the religious fervour of the Scottish Reformation – in which the centuries-old authority of the Roman Catholic Church was challenged by a groundswell of Calvinism, or Protestantism, in 1557 an incendiary covenant was drawn up by a group of powerful nobles known as the Lords of the Congregation.

Supported by the Haldanes, the express aim of the covenant was to 'maintain, set forth and establish the most blessed word of God and his congregation.'

This was at a time when Mary of Guise, mother of Mary, Queen of Scots, ruled as regent in her daughter's name and, as a French Catholic, she became a central target of those seeking religious reform.

To safeguard her rule, but only serving to add fuel to the flames of protest, French troops arrived on Scottish shores and Frenchmen were put in charge of the treasury and given custody of the nation's Great Seal.

As insurrection spread, further inflamed by the fiery preaching of the Protestant reformer John Knox, religious houses were sacked and it was not until 1560 that a truce of sorts was agreed between the Lords of the Congregation and the regent.

Known as the Treaty of Edinburgh, it promised religious toleration and the withdrawal of French troops from the east coast port of Leith, where they had been besieged by forces that included Robert Haldane of Gleneagles and his brother John in the ranks.

But religious unrest continued throughout the following decades and, in 1585, the Haldanes were part of a force that laid siege to Stirling Castle in a bid to persuade the young King James VI to rescind the banishment of a number of dissident nobles who included the Earl of Angus.

Leading an assault on the castle's west port, James Haldane, a brother of the Laird of Gleneagles, was shot and killed after having overcome Sir William Stewart, colonel of the Royal Guard, by Stewart's servant.

The tumultuous seventeenth century saw Haldanes embroiled in the War of the Three Kingdoms of Scotland, England and Ireland.

Also known as the British Civil Wars and of which the English Civil War formed a part, they were sparked off in Scotland during the Bishops' Wars of 1639 and 1640.

The wars had their origin in the widely unpopular attempt by King Charles I to impose uniform religious practice between the Church of England and the proudly independent Scottish Kirk, through the introduction into Scotland of the Episcopal *Book of Common Prayer*.

Flames of unrest were fuelled on Sunday, July 23, 1637 when James Hannay, Dean of Edinburgh, attempted to read from the *Book of Common Prayer* to a packed and surly congregation in St Giles Cathedral.

Incensed by this, Jenny Geddes, a local street trader threw her stool at the hapless minister's head and – translated from Jenny's Old Scots tongue – shouted:

Devil cause you colic in your stomach, false thief: dare you say the Mass in my ear!

This was the signal for a general tumult, as others joined in by lobbing their stools and rioting broke out in the streets.

In turn, this acted as a catalyst for the signing

on February 28, 1638 of the National Covenant – a document as important to Scottish history as the equally famed Declaration of Arbroath of 1320.

Described as 'the glorious marriage day of the kingdom with God', the Covenant renounced Roman Catholic belief, pledged to uphold the Presbyterian religion and called for free parliaments and assemblies.

St Giles Cathedral, Edinburgh

First signed at Edinburgh's Greyfriars Kirk by nobles, barons, burgesses and ministers, it was subscribed to the following day by hundreds of common folk.

Copies were made and dispatched around the nation and subscribed to by thousands more – with its adherents known as Covenanters.

This led to a civil war that raged between Covenanters and Royalists in Scotland from 1638 until 1649, when Charles I was beheaded on the orders of the English Parliament – whose military arm was the New Model Army under Oliver Cromwell.

Although knighted by the ill-fated Charles I in 1633, Sir John Haldane, 11th Laird of Gleneagles and who represented Perth in Parliament, was an ardent supporter of the Covenant and near-bankrupted himself through raising troops and supplies for the cause.

But the political landscape changed following the execution of Charles I and the Scottish Parliament declared his son Charles II 'King of Great Britain, France and Ireland', and duly enthroned him as King of Scots at Scone.

This was only after he reluctantly agreed to the terms of the Covenant and with, it is reasonable to assume, the opportunist monarch's fingers firmly crossed behind his back.

The Scots were now at war with the new Commonwealth of England and, on September 3, 1650, met in battle at Dunbar where Sir John Haldane was killed leading the charge of Clan Haldane.

On a rather more peaceful note, in addition to Gleneagles House another of the historic seats of Clan Haldane is Airthrey Castle – the category B listed building that today forms part of Stirling University campus.

Dating from the eighteenth century and set in magnificent grounds on the outer edge of the Ochil Hills, it had a number of owners until, in 1759, passing into the hands of Captain Robert Haldane who had established a 'great fortune' through service at sea with the East India Company.

Then known as Airthrey House, in 1791 it was rebuilt by his great-nephew, Robert Haldane, 3rd of Airthrey.

Born in 1764 and having served in the Royal Navy, he was described by contemporaries as 'an arrogant, ambitious, purse-proud man' and rather eccentric.

His plans for Airthrey House were certainly

ambitious – commissioning the celebrated architect Robert Adam to rebuild it to a 'castellated villa' design and renaming it Airthrey Castle.

But Haldane baulked at Adam's fee for supervising the building work and, having produced his design, resigned from the rest of the commission.

The building work was carried out and supervised by the master mason Thomas Russell of Edinburgh, while Thomas White of Durham – who had studied under the great English landscape designer Capability Brown – was commissioned to design the grounds of the 363-acre estate.

In keeping with the design for the castle, the design for the grounds was also grand and included a man-made loch that could be used for curling, a hermitage in what became known as Hermitage Wood and a boundary wall nearly four miles in length.

Ever the eccentric, Haldane advertised for a 'full-time hermit' to live in his hermitage. One person applied but, later thinking better of it, declined.

Haldane at one point nearly drowned in his loch, saved only by the timely intervention of local shoemaker Sandy Morrison – whom, contrary to his rather 'purse-proud' character, Haldane rewarded with a lodge in the grounds and a pension for life.

Perhaps it had been because of his narrow escape from drowning and recognition of his own mortality that he appears to have had an almost Damascene conversion, radically altering his lifestyle by devoting himself to evangelical work.

Having built a number of churches and seminaries in Scotland, funded the training of missionaries and funding the Scottish Congregation religious revival, he died in 1842.

His younger brother Captain James Haldane, born in 1768 and better known as the Rev James Haldane, had also served at sea and later pursued a religious vocation – preaching his first sermon in Edinburgh in 1797 and then travelling the country to preach at open-air gatherings and at the Tabernacle Church, now the site of the capital's Playhouse Theatre at the top of Leith Walk.

Founder of the Propagation of the Gospel at Home that organised the publication and distribution of religious tracts, he died in 1851.

Married twice, he had thirteen children who, along with their offspring and succeeding generations of sons, daughters, husbands, wives, uncles, aunts, nephews and nieces constituted a unique family dynasty of high achieving individuals.

Chapter four:

On the world stage

The lives and times of those Haldanes who have gained international distinction are effectively those of the dynasty of the Haldanes of both Gleneagles and Airthrey.

In politics, **Richard Burdon Haldane, 1st Viscount Haldane**, a grandson of the evangelist the Rev James Alexander Haldane, was the influential politician of the early twentieth century responsible, as Secretary of State for War between 1905 and 1912, for army reforms that include the formation of the Territorial Force, better known today as the Territorial Army.

Born in Edinburgh in 1856 and firstly a supporter of the Liberal Party and then the Labour Party, his Haldane reforms to the army also included the establishment of the Officer Training Corps (OTC), while he was raised to the peerage in 1911 as Viscount Haldane, of Cloan in the County of Perth.

Appointed Lord Chancellor in 1912, as war with Germany loomed he was forced to resign the position after falsely and maliciously being accused of harbouring German sympathies.

Also a lawyer, philosopher, author and Fellow of the British Academy, he died in 1928, while he was a younger brother of the pioneering physiologist **John Scott Haldane**.

Born in Edinburgh in 1860 and something of a maverick, many of his important discoveries relating to the functions of the body were made through self-experimentation – such as locking himself in a sealed chamber to determine the effects of potentially lethal combinations of the gaseous elements he breathed in.

Tasked during the First World War with identifying the types of poison gas employed by the Germans, he went on to invent the Black Veil Respirator – the first gas mask.

An authority on the properties of ether, the discoverer of the Haldane Effect on haemoglobin, and a pioneer in the study of pulmonary diseases such as silicosis, he was also responsible for the development of the oxygen tent.

With honours including membership of the Royal Society of Medicine, Royal College of Physicians and founder of the *Journal of Hygiene*, he died in 1936.

Carrying on his legacy, his son John Burdon Sanderson Haldane, better known as **J.B.S. Haldane**, was the physiologist, evolutionary biologist, geneticist and mathematician responsible for a truly astonishing number of breakthroughs in his chosen fields.

In common with his father, Haldane also subjected himself to self-experimentation – on one occasion drinking diluted hydrochloric acid and enclosing himself in an airtight room containing carbon dioxide to test the effects of acidification of the blood.

Many of his discoveries were made while holding academic posts including Fullerian professor of physiology at the Royal Institution, professor of genetics at University College, London and first Weldon professor of biometry at university college.

Coining the words 'clone' and 'cloning' in human biology, helping to create the field of population genetics, establishing human gene 'maps' for haemophilia, discovering how sickle-cell disease can confer some immunity to malaria and a host of other breakthroughs, he was described by the zoologist and cytologist Michael J.D. White as "the most erudite biologist of his generation, and perhaps of the century."

The recipient of honours and awards including the Darwin Medal from the Royal Society and the Kimber Award of the US National Academy of Sciences, shortly before his death from cancer in 1964 he composed the equally famous verse:

> *I know that cancer often kills,*
> *But so do cars and sleeping pills;*
> *And it can hurt one till one sweats,*
> *So can bad teeth and unpaid debts.*
> *A spot of laughter, I am sure,*
> *Often accelerates one's cure;*
> *So let us patients do our bit*
> *To help the surgeons make us fit*

His first wife was the feminist author **Charlotte Haldane** (nee Franken), born in 1894 in Sydenham, Kent.

Married to Haldane from 1926 until they divorced in 1945, she first met him while working as a journalist for the *Daily Express* newspaper.

Describing herself as 'a suffragist and feminist from the age of 16', an advocate of women's rights including divorce reform and easier access to contraception and author of a number of books including her 1927 *Motherhood and its Enemies*, she died in 1969.

A sister of Richard Burdon Haldane, 1st Viscount Haldane, and John Scott Haldane, **Elizabeth Sanderson Haldane** was responsible for the establishment in 1908 of the Voluntary Aid Detachment (VAD).

Born in Edinburgh in 1862 she trained as a nurse and was appointed manager of Edinburgh Royal Infirmary in 1901 and, also a feminist and advocate of women's rights, in 1920 was appointed Scotland's first female Justice of the Peace.

Her autobiography, *From One Century to Another*, covered the period from the year of her birth to the outbreak of the First World War in 1914; she died in 1937.

Another feminist, **Naomi Haldane** was the Scottish novelist and poet better known by her married name **Naomi Mitchison**.

Born in Edinburgh in 1897 and a younger sister of J.B.S. Haldane, she wrote in a variety of genres ranging from historical fiction and poetry to science fiction and travel writing, while as a feminist she was particularly vocal in her campaign for birth control.

Married to the English barrister Gilbert Mitchison, her most controversial work was her 1935 *We Have Been Warned* that, based on a visit to the Soviet Union, examined then taboo subjects such as rape and abortion.

Historical novels include her 1923 *The*

Conquered, the 1925 *Cloud Cuckoo Land* and the 1942 *The Bull Calves* – based on the 1745 Jacobite Rising – while, as a trusted friend of J.R.R. Tolkien she acted as one of the proof readers for his great literary work *The Lord of the Rings*.

Also prominent in the anti-apartheid movement and the recipient of honorary doctorates from a number of universities including Stirling and Strathclyde, she died in 1999.

A son of the Rev James Alexander Haldane through his marriage to his second wife Margaret Rutherford, **Dr Daniel Rutherford Haldane** was the physician born in Edinburgh in 1824.

Resident physician for a time at Edinburgh Royal Infirmary, lecturer at Edinburgh University and having served as president of the Royal College of Physicians of Edinburgh, he died in 1887.

His son, **General Sir James Aylmer Haldane** was the distinguished British Army officer born in 1862.

Commissioned as an officer in the Gordon Highlanders in 1882, he was captured during the Second Boer War of 1899 to 1902 and incarcerated in the same prison camp in Pretoria as fellow officer and future Prime Minister Winston Churchill.

It was Haldane who planned the escape that made Churchill famous, but failed himself in the attempt.

He later complained of how Churchill had been successful without any regard for those such as himself who should have escaped along with him – but Haldane was subsequently successful.

Going on to gain high rank and receiving a number of honours and awards including the Distinguished Service Order (DSO), he died in 1950.

Returning to the world of literature, **Archibald Richard Burdon Haldane** was the social historian and author born in Edinburgh in 1900.

A son of the civil servant and Crown Agent for Scotland Sir William Stowell Haldane and grandson of the Rev James Alexander Haldane, he was the recipient of an honorary doctorate in literature for his major works on the drovers' roads of his native land. Author of books that include his 1944 *The Drove Roads of Scotland* and a number on his passion for trout fishing, including his 1973 *Thirty Years with a Trout Rod*, he died in 1982.

Going back through the centuries and returning to the battlefield, **General Sir George Haldane**, son of Patrick Haldane, 16th Laird of Gleneagles, was the professional soldier who, during the War of the Austrian Succession of 1740 to 1748 fought in June 1743 at the battle of Dettingen, in Bavaria, in the ranks of the British, Hanoverian and Austrian allies – known as the Pragmatic Army – against the French.

The allies were victorious, and General Haldane was also in the ranks when the allies were defeated at the battle of Fontenoy, Belgium, nearly two years later.

The Duke of Cumberland had held command at both battles and General Haldane was also at his side during the abortive Jacobite Rising of 1745 that ended in the carnage of the battle of Culloden in April of 1746.

Later promoted to Brigadier General, after retiring from active military service he served from 1756 until his death in 1759 as governor of Jamaica, where Fort Haldane was erected in his honour.

An establishment figure to the core, he doubtless would have been rather perturbed to learn that one of his direct descendants would be the socialist Jeremy Corbyn, leader of the British Labour Party and Leader of Her Majesty's Opposition in Parliament from 2015 to 2020.